ISBN: 978-1-73429109-4 (Paperback)
ISBN: 978-1-73429108-7 (Hardcover)

Library of Congress Control Number: 2021913755

Any references to historical events, real people, or real places are used fictitiously. Names, characters, and places are products of the author's imagination.

First printing edition 2021
Illustrations, Book Cover Design, and Formatting by SankalpArt
www.sankalpart.com

SheWorks Publishing, LLC
P.O. Box 6402
Newport News, VA 23606

www.sheworkspublishing.com

Dedication

For Ayden & Zoey
For God, Mama Bertha, Papa James, Tierra, Jamie, and Zena, my
most significant pillars of love;
and for You, the phenomenal breadth of life reading this:
May you conquer any challenge that comes your way.

Theron C. Sampson

Cedric's Quest: Conquering Phonics in the 21st Century

Directions: Parents or teachers, read each page to the child as they listen and follow along. As their phonics fluency increases, have them read aloud to you.

Before we begin, let's review what CVC words are. CVC words begin with a consonant, have a vowel in the middle, and have a consonant at the end. Consonants are the letters b, c, d, f, g, h, j, k, l, m, n, p, q, r, s, t, v, w, x, y, and z. Vowels are the letters a, e, i, o, and u, and sometimes y. An example of a CVC word is <u>dog</u>.
(Consonant = d, vowel = o, consonant = g)

This BooK Belongs to:

....

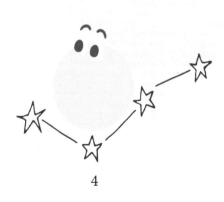

"Ring, ring, ring!" is all little Cedric could hear as he opened his eyes.

It was his parents' alarm clock
ringing to wake them up.

6

Cedric could hear his mother and father walking down the hallway. "Time to wake up, Cedric," they called from the hallway.

"We are going into the city today to <u>RUN</u> errands and take you and your sister shopping," said <u>MOM.</u>

"While we are shopping today, you will practice for your virtual quiz on recognizing and sounding out CVC words," said DAD.

Little Cedric was nervous because CVC words were hard. Being away from school and learning from home because of the coronavirus pandemic was also hard for him.

10

He was away from his friends at school and could only see them three times a week. The other two days, Cedric would see his friends in class from his laptop.

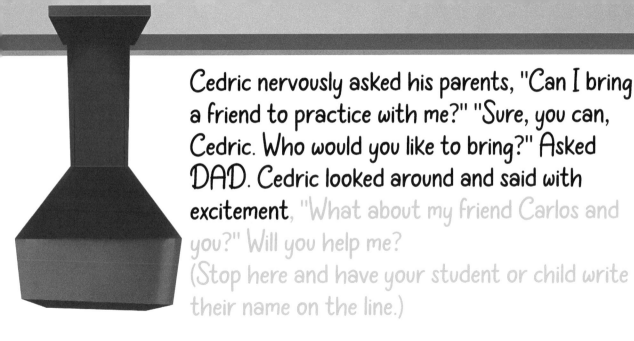

Cedric nervously asked his parents, "Can I bring a friend to practice with me?" "Sure, you can, Cedric. Who would you like to bring?" Asked DAD. Cedric looked around and said with excitement, "What about my friend Carlos and you?" Will you help me?
(Stop here and have your student or child write their name on the line.)

....

12

Directions: In the upcoming sections, as you read to, or with, the child, put emphasis on each underlined letter in the word. The child should sound out each letter and blend the sound to say the word. Assist the child with sounding out each letter sound and word if they are having difficulty. Have them use their finger to follow along as you read.

Cedric <u>PUT</u> on his clothes. He went downstairs to <u>EAT</u> with his family. Cedric's mom <u>SAT</u> at the stove, making him his favorite, bacon, and eggs. "Come on in and <u>SIT</u> down. Your breakfast is almost ready," she said.

Cedric's sister, Tierra, RAN downstairs and SAT down beside him. They smiled as they finished eating their food. "Okay, children, time to GET ready," said their father. "As you two GET ready, I will MOP the floor," said their mother.

CEDRIC

TIERRA

As Cedric and his sister went to their rooms, they made
sure to <u>PET</u> the <u>DOG.</u> Cedric <u>PUT</u> on his shirt and made
sure to <u>ZIP</u> up his pants.

His mother called from downstairs, "When you all are ready, do <u>NOT</u> come into the kitchen. The floor will still be <u>WET</u>."

16

Once they were all ready, they all GOT into the CAR.

"Hey, everyone, before we pull off, don't forget to <u>PUT</u> your mask in your pockets," said their mother. "We want to stay safe while we are outside today. Make sure your nose and lips are covered."

While driving into the city, Cedric's father looked in the rearview mirror. He <u>SAW</u> Cedric leaning in the seat with his <u>HAT</u> over his head. "Cedric, <u>SIT</u> up straight and turn off your tablet," said his father.

"You have to continue reading with your friend, _____ (Stop here and have your student or child write their name on the line again). You don't want them to be <u>SAD</u>," he said. Cedric replied, "I'm excited to have your help!"

Cedric took his <u>HAT</u> off of his head. As he looked out the window, he could feel the <u>SUN</u> shining on his face.

21

It was HOT outside today. So his parents PUT the FAN on to keep everyone cool.

22

Cedric and his sister could hear RAP music from a CAR coming down the street.

They began to TAP their feet on the floor as the CAR passed by them.

15

24

They arrived at the store. <u>DAD</u> said, "Okay, we are here, everyone. Cedric and Tierra, please remember to walk, and do not <u>RUN</u> in the shopping center."

25

Cedric looked to his friend, ...
(Your child's/student's name written here).
"This is going to be so much FUN!" he said with
excitement in his voice.

"Cedric, will you grab a cart?" <u>MOM</u> asked. Cedric <u>RAN</u> to the carts and broke the first rule <u>DAD</u> said <u>NOT</u> to do when inside the shopping center.

"I am sorry, DAD. I will NOT do that again," Cedric said. Then, with a frown on his face, DAD said, "Cedric, remember to follow the rules we went over before coming into the store."

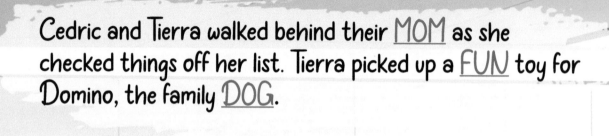

Cedric and Tierra walked behind their <u>MOM</u> as she checked things off her list. Tierra picked up a <u>FUN</u> toy for Domino, the family <u>DOG</u>.

She asked DAD, "Can you buy this TOY so Domino and I can RUN and play the fetch game?" DAD said, "Yes, sure we can, Tierra. PUT it in the cart along with the other items."

30

MOM looked at the cart and said, "Okay, everyone, no more extra items in the cart. We cannot FIT anything else in the cart."

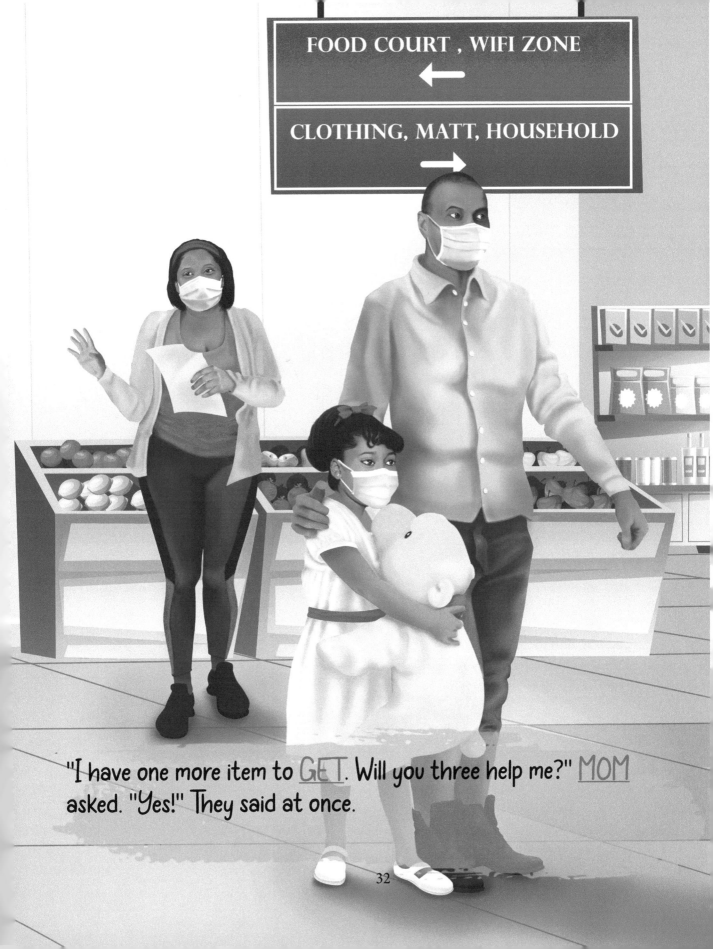

"I have one more item to GET. Will you three help me?" MOM asked. "Yes!" They said at once.

"Perfect! We need a new <u>MAT</u> for the <u>DOG</u>," <u>MOM</u> said.

While looking around the store, DAD found a BIG, blue, fluffy MAT. DAD took the MAT back to the shopping cart for everyone to see. They all were excited about the new MAT for the family DOG.

34

MOM yelled out, "We are done shopping!" "That was FUN!" Tierra shouted. "Now, time for a NAP for me!" said their mother. Cedric said to his MOM, "But the SUN is still out." "I know, Cedric, but all of this shopping has made me tired," MOM said as she yawned.

"Well, time to go, Cedric, Tierra, and.......................................
(Stop here and have your student or child write their name on the line again.)." With excitement, Cedric shouted, "Thank you for helping me conquer my fear of Phonics!

"When we work together and believe in ourselves, we can do anything!"

The End

36

CVC Vocabulary List

BOY	HOT	SAW
BIG	MOM	SIT
CAR	MOP	SUN
DAD	NAP	TAP
DOG	NOT	TOP
EAT	PET	WET
FAN	PUT	ZIP
FIT	RAN	
FUN	RAP	
GET	RUN	
GOT	SAD	
HAT		

37

Acknowledgments

Thank you to my wife, daughter, family, friends, and staff members for your continued support in my quest to ensure every child has an opportunity to drink from the fountain of knowledge. Thank you to my team of people who have helped me through this process:
Shernika Battle, Zena Sampson, James Sampson,
Bertha Sampson, Tierra Sampson, Dr. Edith Rudd, and, most importantly, God for guiding me to write this book.

About Author

Theron Sampson is a native of Richmond, Virginia. He is a Public School - Principal dedicated to ensuring children receive a quality education and the support necessary to succeed. Positive collaboration is his approach toward the fields of education and leadership.

This book was born out of his desire to have children learn foundational reading skills while conquering their fears of reading. He has a relentless passion for ensuring every child has an opportunity to drink from the fountain of knowledge. He mentors students, volunteers in the community, and sharpens his educational expertise in his spare time. This is his first book.